Dark Side of the Spoon
The Rock Cookbook

Published in 2017 by
Laurence King Publishing Ltd
361–373 City Road
London EC1V 1LR
e-mail: enquiries@laurenceking.com
www.laurenceking.com

Editors: Joseph Inniss, Ralph Miller and Peter Stadden
Text: Joseph Inniss and Ralph Miller
Graphic design: Peter Stadden

A catalogue record for this book is available from the British Library.
ISBN 978-1-78627-089-4

Printed in China

Dark Side of the Spoon
The Rock Cookbook

INNISS, MILLER & STADDEN

Intro

Great recipes are a lot like the best rock bands. They've got to be crowd-pleasing, with a touch of bravado, and can be enhanced with a flash of improvisation. Every ingredient in a recipe has its own important part to play to deliver a truly memorable performance. Whether you're cooking up a mean solo, or jamming in a group, *Dark Side of the Spoon: The Rock Cookbook* will cater for all tastes.

Rock 'n' roll is littered with culinary links, from Guns N' Roses' *Appetite for Destruction*, to System of a Down's *Chop Suey* and Ozzy Osbourne biting the head off a bat (rest assured, there are no bat recipes here). This book aims to further bridge the gap between food and rock.

This is our second pun-tastic recipe book following on from *Rapper's Delight: The Hip Hop Cookbook*. This time around, we are celebrating the best of rock with easy-to-cook dishes. Each recipe is inspired by rock legends past and present, and is accompanied by an illustration created exclusively for the book by our favorite artists.

Dark Side of the Spoon contains 30 delicious recipes devised for cooks of all abilities. Some dishes are like a catchy riff—simple, but effective; while others are like listening to an epic LP— complex, longer-lasting, but hugely rewarding.

We've designed this book to be as accessible as possible, and nothing should be too tricky for any cook with an open mind. The volume dial on each spread shows how much culinary skill will be required to serve up your festival of flavors (like Spinal Tap's amp, this goes up to 11). The B.P.M. (or Beats Per Minute) scale indicates how long each recipe takes to prepare and cook.

All recipes serve four people, but can easily be scaled down or up by increasing or decreasing the ingredients, so it won't matter how many groupies you're catering for.

The Equipment Matrix on pages 8–9 tells you exactly what you'll need before you start cooking. The Supporting Acts section includes our favorite accompaniments to help turn your meal into a feast. There's also an Advanced Methods section (pages 84–87), for those of you who are more confident in the kitchen, or want to try something a little more ambitious.

We hope this book will entertain and elevate you to rock-god status in the kitchen. Bon appetit!

The Dark Side of the Spoon team
darksideofthespooncookbook.com

Contents

Contents

Contents

Equipment Matrix

This is a list of equipment that you might need to cook the dishes in this book. For most recipes we assume you have standard kitchen equipment such as saucepans, skillets, mixing bowls, a colander, a kitchen scale, and an oven, but this matrix is designed to highlight more unusual things you might need for specific recipes.

Preparation

Fleetwood Mac & Cheese	
Pig Floyd	
Tofu Fighters	
Beef Patty Smith	
Captain Beeftart	
Suzi Quatro Formaggi	
Slip Gnocchi	
Status Pho	
The Offspring Rolls	
Dim Sum 41	
Tex-Mex Pistols	
Mötley Stüe	
ZZ Top	
Metallikatsu Curry	
Ramenstein	
Smoked Haddock on the Water	
Ladle of Filth	
Primal Bream	
Def Sheppard	
Limp Brisket	
Iron Raisin	
Slayer Cake	
The Rolling Scones	
Smashing Pumpkin Pie	
Nirvana Split	
Spinal Tapioca	
Dire Dates	
Sepultempura Fried Ice Cream	
Judas Peach	
Whitesnaked Alaska	

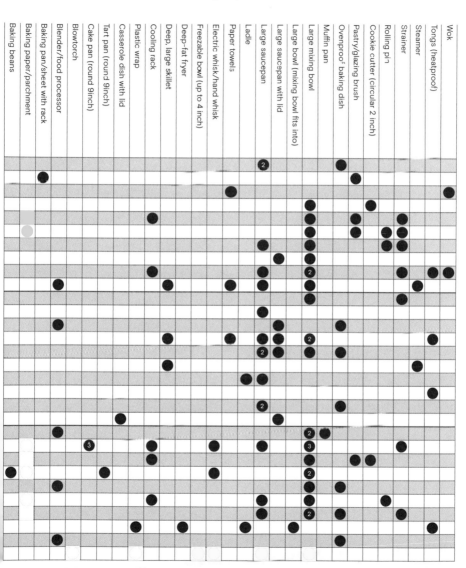

Preparation

Fleetwood Mac & Cheese

You Can Cook Your Own Way (... but we suggest this way)

Appetizers

Difficulty

Description

Crispy cauliflower macaroni and cheese.

B.P.M.

25 minutes preparation
25 minutes cooking

Ingredients

1 cauliflower
14oz elbow macaroni
A drop of olive oil
2 oz (½ stick) butter
4 tablespoons all-purpose flour
1½ cups whole milk
7 oz extra sharp Cheddar cheese, grated (about 2¼ cups)
1 teaspoon Dijon mustard
Salt and freshly ground black pepper

Method

1. Trim the leaves and stalk from the cauliflower and cut the head into quarters.
2. Put the cauliflower quarters in a large saucepan of boiling water with the macaroni. Add a pinch of salt and the olive oil to prevent the macaroni pieces sticking together. Cook for 20 minutes until the cauliflower breaks up.
3. While the pasta and cauliflower are cooking pre-heat the oven to 400°F and make the cheese sauce.
4. Melt the butter in a saucepan over medium heat, then add 2 tablespoons of the flour and whisk.
5. Add the rest of the flour half a tablespoon at a time to ensure there are no lumps. When you have made a rough paste, gradually add the milk, whisking continuously to make the mixture as smooth as possible. Cook the sauce, stirring, for 3–4 minutes until it has thickened.
6. Add a scant 1½ cups of the Cheddar cheese and whisk until smooth. Add the mustard and stir until thoroughly combined.
7. Drain the cauliflower and pasta through a colander, and break up the cauliflower (it should break up even more, into smaller pieces).
8. Place the macaroni and cauliflower mixture in an ovenproof baking dish and pour the Cheddar cheese sauce over it, then add a pinch of salt and black pepper and mix together.
9. Sprinkle over the remaining Cheddar cheese.
10. Place in the oven and bake for 25 minutes until the top is crisp and golden. If you want it extra crispy, you can turn on the broiler setting at the end for a few minutes.

Pig Floyd

Comfortably Yum

Appetizers

Difficulty

Description

Homemade spicy pork rinds, served with wholegrain mustard.

B.P.M.

10 minutes preparation
25 minutes cooking

Ingredients

9 oz pork rind (crackling)
(see note below)
2 teaspoons fine salt
2 teaspoons ground cumin
1 teaspoon dried red pepper flakes
3 tablespoons white wine vinegar
2–3 teaspoons whole grain mustard

Note: Pork rinds can be purchased from some butchers, or Latino or Asian food markets

Method

1. Preheat the oven to its highest setting.
2. Slice or cut the pork rind into thin strips (you may find it easier to cut with scissors), about the width of your thumb and the length of your finger.
3. Lay out the slices of rind on a rack on your baking pan, skin-side up.
4. Sprinkle the salt, ground cumin, and dried chili flakes over the rinds.
5. Pour the white wine vinegar into a small bowl and dab the rinds with the white wine vinegar using a pastry brush (be careful not to knock the seasoning off the rinds).
6. Place the baking pan in the oven and cook the rinds for 20 minutes (as they cook and crisp up, the rinds will curve and bend). After 20 minutes, turn the rinds over so the skin is at the bottom and the fat is at the top, and cook for an additional 5 minutes.
7. Remove from the oven and serve on a plate or board with the whole grain mustard.

Tofu Fighters

Learn To Fry

Difficulty

Description

Honey and ginger tofu stir-fry.

B.P.M.

5 minutes preparation
20 minutes cooking

Ingredients

7 oz firm beancurd (tofu)
1 teaspoon cornstarch
A pinch of salt
3 tablespoons sunflower oil
2 tablespoons runny honey
2 garlic cloves
2-inch piece of fresh ginger
8 scallions
2 red chilies
1 yellow bell pepper
1 lime
1 tablespoon soy sauce
2 tablespoons sesame seeds

Method

1. Cut the tofu into 1-inch cubes, put them in a bowl, add the cornstarch and salt and toss to combine.
2. Place some paper towels on a plate (this is to absorb the excess oil from the tofu).
3. Heat the sunflower oil in a wok on the highest heat possible for 2 minutes.
4. Add the tofu to the wok and cook, stirring frequently, for about 6 minutes until golden and crisp.
5. Remove the wok from the heat, and scoop the tofu out and onto the paper towels to drain away excess oil. Leave the rest of the oil in the wok.
6. Put the tofu into a bowl and drizzle the honey over it.
7. Peel and dice the garlic. Peel the ginger, and slice it into fine strips.
8. Cut away the roots from the scallions then cut into 1½-inch batons. Cut the chilies and the bell pepper in half, scrape away the seeds, then cut them into thin strips. Cut the lime in half and set it aside.
9. Place the wok over medium heat and allow the oil to heat for 30 seconds.
10. Add the garlic, ginger, scallions, chilies, and pepper and cook for 5 minutes, stirring constantly.
11. Squeeze the juice from both halves of the lime into the wok, and add the soy sauce.
12. Divide the mixture from the wok into bowls, then distribute the tofu between the bowls, placing it on top of the mixture. To finish, sprinkle half a tablespoon of sesame seeds over each serving.

Beef Patty Smith

Because The Night Belongs To Burgers

Difficulty

Description

Burger sliders served with greens and Cheddar cheese.

B.P.M.

15 minutes preparation
15 minutes cooking

Ingredients

4-6 hamburger buns
3 garlic cloves
1 red onion
1 tablespoon butter
18 oz ground beef
A pinch of salt
1 teaspoon ground
black pepper
1 teaspoon dried red pepper
flakes
2 teaspoons hot smoked
paprika
1½ teaspoons ground
coriander
1 egg
3½ oz sharp Cheddar cheese
1 tablespoon olive oil
A handful of lettuce leaves

Method

1. Use a 2-inch cookie cutter to cut your hamburger buns into small discs. (If you do not have a cookie cutter, use a small cup as a template, and cut around it.) Cut the discs in half to make 12 thin mini burger buns and set aside.
2. Peel and dice the garlic and red onion.
3. Place the butter in a skillet over low heat.
4. Put the garlic and onion in the skillet with the butter and cook for 4-5 minutes until softened, not browned, then remove from the heat and transfer to a bowl to cool for around 5 minutes.
5. Place the beef in a mixing bowl, add the salt and black pepper, paprika, and ground coriander, and a few sprinkles of the red pepper flakes.
6. Crack the egg into a small bowl and beat it, then add it to the beef mixture.
7. Add the onion and garlic to the beef.
8. Using your hands, bring the mixture together to form a large ball.

9. Break off small chunks of the mixture, about the size of the palm of your hand. Roll these chunks into balls then flatten them to make patties. This mixture should make around 12 2-inch patties. Ensure the patties are tightly squished together so they won't fall apart in the pan.
10. Cut the Cheddar cheese into small chunks, and set them aside to add to the sliders later. Place the skillet over the heat and drizzle with the oil.
11. Place the patties in the skillet and cook them for 5-7 minutes until they brown—turning them so they brown on both sides. Cook them for longer if you prefer your beef well-done.
12. Once the patties are all cooked, build your sliders: place lettuce leaves on one half of a bun, add the beef patties and chunks of cheese, then top with the other bun half. Repeat with the remaining patties and buns.

Captain Beeftart

Observatory Crust

Difficulty

Description

Puff pastry beef tart
with hints of chocolate
and cinnamon.

B.P.M.

40 minutes preparation
30 minutes cooking

Ingredients

9 oz salad tomatoes
1 tablespoon olive oil
10½ oz lean ground beef
2 tablespoons all-purpose
flour
5¾ oz sheet of puff pastry
2 tablespoons ground
cinnamon
¾ oz dark chocolate
1 egg

Method

1. Preheat the oven to
425°F.
2. Dice half the tomatoes
and set them aside with the
remaining tomatoes (leave
these whole).
3. Place a skillet over high
heat and add the olive oil.
4. Add the ground beef to
the pan and cook it for
10 minutes until browned,
breaking up clumps of meat
with a wooden spoon.
5. Transfer the beef from the
pan to a strainer, and leave
to drain over the sink for 10
minutes. This is important as
it prevents the pastry from
going mushy later.
6. Line 2 baking sheets with
parchment paper, then dust
them with half the flour.
7. Dust a clean work surface
with the rest of the flour and
lay out the puff pastry, then
cut it into quarters. Place
the pastry pieces on the
baking sheets, leaving space
between each piece.
8. Combine the ground beef
and diced tomato in a mixing
bowl, stirring thoroughly.

9. Leaving a 1-inch gap
around the edge of each
pastry sheet, top the pastry
sheets with the beef and
tomato mixture.
10. Evenly dust the beef with
the ground cinnamon, then
grate the dark chocolate
over the beef.
11. Slice the remaining
tomatoes into strips with
a sharp knife, as thinly as
possible, and lay these over
the beef.
12. Crack the egg into a bowl
and beat with a fork, then
brush the exposed pastry
edges with the beaten egg
using a pastry brush.
13. Place the baking sheets
in the center of the
preheated oven and bake
for 20 minutes.
14. Remove the tarts from
the oven, and leave them to
cool on a cooling rack for
5 minutes before eating.

Tom Newell

Suzi Quatro Formaggi
Devil Grated Drive

Difficulty

Description
Four mini cheese pizzas.

B.P.M.
1 hour 25 minutes preparation
15 minutes cooking

Ingredients
1 cup + 3 tablespoons white bread flour (plus extra to dust)
1 teaspoon instant dry yeast
½ teaspoon salt
½ teaspoon superfine sugar
1 tablespoon olive oil
2 tablespoons milk
1 tablespoon polenta (cornmeal) for rolling
2 garlic cloves
2oz (½ stick) butter
2 sprigs of thyme
4½oz mozzarella ball
1¾oz blue cheese
3½oz sharp Cheddar cheese
1¾oz Parmesan cheese
Freshly ground black pepper

Method
1. Sift the flour into a mixing bowl and add the yeast to one side of the bowl and the salt and sugar to the other.
2. Make a well in the center and add the olive oil.
3. Heat the milk in a bowl in the microwave, or a pan on the stovetop, until lukewarm. Gradually add the milk to the flour.
4. Pour a scant ½ cup warm water into the flour and mix with your hands until the ingredients come together to form a stiff dough.
5. Dust the work surface with a tablespoon of the bread flour and turn out the dough.
6. Knead the dough for 5 minutes, then roll it into a ball.
7. Cover the dough with the large bowl, and leave it to rise for 1 hour and 15 minutes, or until doubled in size.
8. Once the dough has risen, preheat the oven to 425°F and line a baking sheet with parchment paper.
9. Sprinkle the work surface with the polenta.
10. Place the dough on the

surface and punch it to knock out the air. Knead for around 1 minute, then shape into a ball.
11. Divide the ball into 4 pieces. Dust your rolling pin with polenta, and roll each piece into a flat base, stretch the bases out as thinly as possible, then place them on the lined baking sheet.
12. Peel and dice the garlic and place it in a bowl with the butter. Melt in the microwave (or saucepan) for 30 seconds.
13. Chop the leaves from the sprigs of thyme, and add them to the melted butter.
14. Spread the butter, garlic, and thyme mixture over the bases with a pastry brush.
15. Slice the mozzarella ball and divide it between the bases.
16. Slice the blue cheese and divide it between the bases.
17. Grate the Cheddar and the Parmesan and sprinkle them over the bases.
18. Bake for around 15 minutes, or until the base turns golden.
19. Remove from the oven, serve on a plate and sprinkle with black pepper to taste.

Slip Gnocchi

Don't Spit It Out

Appetizers

Difficulty

Description

Italian gnocchi *aglio e olio* (garlic and oil)—spicy chili and garlic pasta dough dumplings.

B.P.M.

15 minutes preparation
1 hour 10 minutes cooking

Ingredients

18 oz potatoes
2 large eggs
A pinch of salt
1⅓ cups all-purpose flour (you may need more for dusting)
4½ tablespoons olive oil
5 garlic cloves
2 teaspoons red pepper flakes
3½ oz Parmesan cheese
Freshly ground black pepper

Method

For the gnocchi:
1. Place the potatoes (skin on) in a saucepan with water and bring to a boil.
2. Once boiling, reduce the heat, and simmer for 50 minutes. Preheat the oven to 400°F.
3. When they are cooked, drain them, place them on a baking sheet and cook in the oven for 10 minutes.
5. Remove the potatoes from the oven, halve them, and scoop the potato out of the skins.
6. Put the potato in the empty saucepan and mash, then pass through a strainer into a large mixing bowl to ensure finely mashed potato.
7. Crack the eggs into the mixing bowl with the potato and add the salt.
8. Add 1⅛ cups of the flour and mix to form a dough.
9. Dust the work surface with the remaining flour, tip out the dough, and bring it together to form a ball.
10. Roll the dough into a long, thin snake shape, then chop into small, thumb-sized segments. The gnocchi is ready to cook. (If you're not cooking them immediately, dust them with flour to stop them sticking.)
11. Place the gnocchi in a large pan of boiling water, and add half a tablespoon of the olive oil to prevent sticking.
12. Boil for about 3 minutes—when ready, the gnocchi will float to the surface. Drain the gnocchi in a colander.
For the aglio e olio:
1. Peel and dice the garlic.
2. Heat the rest of the oil in a skillet over high heat, add the garlic and the red pepper flakes and fry for 2–3 minutes.
3. Remove from the heat, and add the gnocchi, stirring to ensure the gnocchi is coated in the sauce, then tip them into a serving bowl. Drizzle over the remaining contents of the skillet.
4. Grate the Parmesan over the dish, and season with black pepper to taste.

Status Pho

Rockin' All Over The Bowl

Appetizers

Difficulty

6

Description

Traditional Vietnamese beef pho stock with rice noodles.

B.P.M.

15 minutes preparation
4 hours 15 minutes cooking

Ingredients

1 onion
3-inch piece of fresh ginger
8½ cups pho bone stock*
(optional)
1 lb oxtail
1 package Pho spice*
14 oz sirloin steak (approx. 2 steaks)
8 oz instant rice noodles
1 lime

Method

For the broth:

1. Peel the onion and cut it into quarters. Peel the ginger and cut it into small chunks.
2. Place a skillet over high heat (don't add any oil).
3. Place the onion and ginger chunks in the skillet and fry for 10 minutes, turning them every minute or so.
4. After 10 minutes, the outside of the onion should be lightly charred (don't worry if the ginger doesn't char). Remove from the heat and transfer the onion and ginger to a saucepan.
5. If you're using your own pho bone stock* add this to the saucepan. Otherwise, add 8½ cups water to the saucepan and bring to a boil.
6. Reduce the heat to a simmer, and add the oxtail and the pho spice.
7. Cover the pan with a lid, and leave to simmer over low heat for 4 hours. Once cooked, follow the next steps to make the pho.

For the pho:

1. Place a large heatproof bowl under a colander and tip in the contents of the saucepan—discard the solids in the colander.
2. Transfer the liquid back into the saucepan, and place over low heat to simmer.
3. Slice the steak into thin strips and set aside.
4. Boil a kettle full of water. Put the rice noodles into a heatproof bowl and cover with boiling water. Leave to stand for 3 minutes.
5. Drain and rinse the rice noodles, then divide between 4 serving bowls. Divide the broth between the 4 bowls, pouring it over the noodles.
6. Divide the steak between the 4 bowls, laying them out on top of the rice noodles. Leave the noodles and steak to stand for 2 minutes. Add a wedge of lime to each bowl before serving.

*See Advanced Methods p84 to make your own pho spice mix and pho bone stock.

The Offspring Rolls

Pretty Fly For A Light Fry

Appetizers

Difficulty

Description

Vegetarian fried Chinese spring rolls (makes 8).

B.P.M.

20 minutes preparation
5 minutes cooking

Ingredients

1-inch piece of fresh ginger
1 garlic clove
4½ oz napa cabbage
4½ oz carrots
3 oz shiitake mushrooms
A handful of mint leaves
A handful of cilantro leaves
5 tablespoons sunflower oil
2 oz instant rice noodles
3 oz beansprouts
1 teaspoon soy sauce
1 tablespoon cornstarch
8 spring roll wrappers (of the pastry variety, not rice paper)
Sweet chili dipping sauce* (optional)

Method

1. Peel and slice the ginger into thin strips. Peel and dice the garlic.
2. Slice the cabbage, carrots (peeled), and mushrooms into thin strips. Chop the herbs.
3. Add 1 tablespoon of the oil to a wok, then place the wok on the highest heat possible for 2 minutes. Add the cabbage, carrots, mushrooms, ginger, and garlic and stir-fry for 4 minutes.
4. Remove the wok from the heat and tip the mixture into a bowl to cool.
5. Boil a kettle full of water. Put the rice noodles into a heatproof bowl and cover with boiling water. Leave to stand for 3 minutes.
6. Drain the noodles and rinse them. Drain again, and return to the bowl.
7. Add the cabbage, carrots, mushrooms, ginger, and garlic to the noodles, then add the beansprouts, mint, cilantro, and soy sauce. Mix together.
8. Mix the cornstarch in a bowl with 2 tablespoons of water to make a paste.

9. Place a spring roll wrapper on a flat surface, then place one-eighth of the filling in the center, leaving a space of about 2 inches between the filling and edge of the wrap.
10. Fold over one side of the wrap to cover the filling, then dab cornstarch paste onto the edges of the wrap. Fold in the ends of the wrap, then roll it into a neat, sealed roll (the pastry must be sealed to prevent them breaking apart while frying). Repeat with the rest of the wraps and filling.
11. Wipe the wok clean, add the remaining oil, and place over high heat.
12. When the oil is hot, place the rolls in the wok one at a time (avoid them touching each other), and fry them for 3–4 minutes, turning them with tongs until golden brown.
13. Cool the rolls on a cooling rack, then serve with sweet chili dipping sauce* (if using).

*See Advanced Methods p85 to make your own sweet chili dipping sauce.

Dim Sum 41

All Filler No Killer

Difficulty

(7)

Description

Small plates of Chinese shrimp dumplings and shrimp toast served with a spicy sauce.

B.P.M.

30 minutes preparation
8 minutes cooking

Ingredients

1 red chili, finely diced
3 tablespoons sesame oil
3 tablespoons soy sauce
A handful of beansprouts
1 teaspoon superfine sugar
½ teaspoon salt
1½ tablespoons rice wine
18 oz raw peeled shrimps
1 package of dumpling pastry
3 scallions
2 garlic cloves
1 large egg
2 teaspoons cornstarch
1 teaspoon hot chili sauce
4 slices of white bread
¼ cup sesame seeds
1¼ cups sunflower oil

Method

For the dumpling sauce:
1. Halve and seed the chili, dice it, and fry it in a skillet with 1 tablespoon of the sesame oil for 1 minute.
2. Tip the chili into a bowl. Add the soy sauce and mix.
For the dumplings:
1. Finely chop the beansprouts and fry them in a skillet with 1 tablespoon of the sesame oil for 3 minutes until golden, then remove from the heat and tip into a bowl.
2. Sprinkle the superfine sugar and the salt over the beansprouts and stir.
3. Add another tablespoon of sesame oil and all the rice wine.
4. Blend half the shrimp in a food processor until smooth, add to the beansprout mixture and stir.
5. Take a piece of dumpling pastry, place some shrimp mix in the middle, then fold over and seal the parcels with damp fingers. Repeat with the remaining pastry and filling.
6. Pour boiling water into the base of a steamer. Place the dumplings in the steamer and

cover. Steam for 5 minutes, then transfer the dumplings to a dry skillet and fry over medium heat for a minute to crisp up.
For the shrimp toast:
1. Cut the scallions into chunks and peel the garlic.
2. Put the remaining shrimp in a blender and add the scallions and garlic.
3. Yolk an egg* then pour the white into the blender.
4. Add the cornstarch and chili sauce, then blend the mixture to make a thick paste.
5. Cut the bread slices diagonally to create triangles.
6. Spread the shrimp paste on the triangles so it covers the bread and sprinkle over the sesame seeds.
7. Heat the sunflower oil in a deep saucepan for 2–3 minutes over high heat.
8. Drop in the bread and cook until brown, turning them once.
9. Place on paper towels to soak up excess oil, then serve with the dumplings and sauce.

*See Advanced Methods p85.

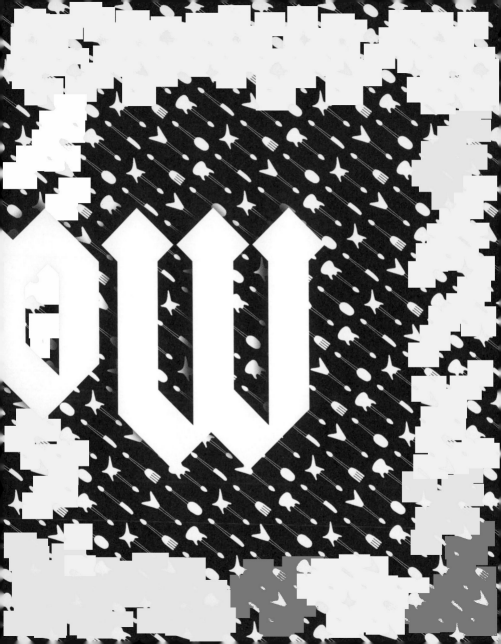

Tex-Mex Pistols

God Save The Bean

Difficulty

Description

Fajita steak and kidney bean tortilla wraps.

B.P.M.

15 minutes preparation
15 minutes cooking

Ingredients

1 lb flank steak
Package of fajita seasoning*
1 red bell pepper, halved and seeded
1 yellow bell pepper, halved and seeded
4 small tortilla wraps
1 tablespoon olive oil
1 red onion, diced
14 oz canned red kidney beans, drained
8 large leaves iceberg lettuce
1 tablespoon sour cream

Notes

Any type of frying steak will do, but flank has the most authentic Tex-Mex flavor.

Method

1. Slice the steak into thin strips (about ⅓ inch thick) and place in a bowl.
2. Add half the fajita seasoning to the steaks and gently rub the seasoning into the meat with your hands, then set aside.
3. Slice both the peppers into strips (about ¼ inch thick).
4. Preheat the oven to its lowest heat.
5. Place the tortilla wraps on a baking sheet, then place the sheet in the oven.
6. Place serving plates on the bottom shelf of the oven.
7. Heat the oil in a skillet over high heat.
8. Drain and rinse the kidney beans using a strainer, add to the skillet with the onion, pepper, and remaining fajita seasoning, and cook for 5 minutes, stirring continuously.
9. Add the strips of steak to the skillet, and cook for an additional 5 minutes, turning them occasionally.
10. Lay a tortilla wrap on each of the preheated serving plates. Tear 8 large leaves from the lettuce, then place 2 leaves on each tortilla, and add a dollop of the sour cream to each tortilla.
11. Divide the fajita steak strips and beans between each wrap, then roll up the wraps and serve.

*See Advanced Methods p86 to make your own spicy fajita seasoning.

Mains

Mötley Stüe

with Tommy Leeks

Mains

Difficulty

Description

A warming vegetarian winter stew with "melt your face off" Gruyère cheese.

B.P.M.

10 minutes preparation
35 minutes cooking

Ingredients

1 leek
3 carrots
5 new potatoes (skin on)
3 tablespoons olive oil
1 pot of vegetable stock
(approx. 1 oz)
A sprig of rosemary
A handful of flat-leaf parsley
2½ oz Gruyère cheese
7 oz fresh spinach
Freshly ground black pepper
Sliced bread, to serve
(optional)

Method

1. Trim the leek and cut it into thin disks.
2. Peel the carrots and cut them into small chunks, and cut the potatoes (skin on) into small chunks.
3. Heat the oil in the saucepan over medium heat, add the leek and cook for 5–10 minutes. The leek should reduce down and start to brown.
4. Boil a kettle full of water, then mix 2½ cups of boiling water with the vegetable stock pot in a heatproof measuring cup.
5. Once the leek has started to brown, pour in the stock, then add the potatoes and carrots, and simmer for 20 minutes.
6. Strip the leaves off the rosemary sprig, and sprinkle them into the saucepan.
7. Tear a few leaves of flat-leaf parsley, and sprinkle them into the saucepan.
8. While the stew is bubbling away, grate the Gruyère cheese into a bowl.
9. Place the spinach on top of the stew—it will gradually wilt. Once it has fully wilted, stir it into the stew.
10. Add the grated cheese to the stew, stir thoroughly, and cook for an additional 2 minutes.
11. Serve the stew hot, in bowls, and add black pepper to taste. Serve with sliced bread, if you like.

ZZ Chop

Sharp Dressed Lamb

Mains

Difficulty

Description

Lamb chops with lime-mint sauce, served with rice.

B.P.M.

30 minutes preparation
40 minutes cooking

Ingredients

3 onions
7 oz carrots
2 tablespoons sunflower oil
8 lamb chops
(approx. 18 oz)
4 large sprigs of thyme
2 limes
1 small jalapeño pepper
1½ tablespoons honey
1½ tablespoons white
wine vinegar
A handful of mint leaves
2 tablespoons olive oil
1⅛ cups basmati rice

Method

For the lamb:
1. Preheat the oven to 400°F.
2. Peel the onions and cut two of them into rough quarters. Peel the carrots and cut them into 2-inch batons.
3. Pour the sunflower oil into an ovenproof baking dish, and place the lamb chops in the center. Surround the lamb with the quartered onions, carrots, and thyme. Bake in the oven for 40 minutes. While the lamb is cooking, prepare the sauce. Start cooking the rice 15 minutes before the lamb is ready.
For the lime-mint sauce:
1. Cut the 2 limes in half and squeeze the juice of both into a blender.
2. Remove the stalk from the jalapeño pepper. Add the honey, jalapeño pepper, white wine vinegar, and mint leaves to the blender and blitz. Pour into a dish and set aside.
For the rice:
1. Boil a kettle full of water (at least 2½ cups). Dice the third onion.
2. Place a saucepan over high

heat and add the olive oil, then add the onion, and stir for 2 minutes.
3. Add the rice to the saucepan, and stir to evenly coat the rice in the olive oil.
4. Pour 2½ cups of boiling water over the rice and onion. Do not stir the rice again. Cover the saucepan with a lid, and reduce the heat to a simmer. Allow the rice to cook, covered, for 8 minutes, then remove from the heat.
5. To serve, place 2 lamb chops on each plate with the onions and carrots.
6. Divide the rice between the plates and pour the lime-mint sauce over the lamb chops.

Metallikatsu Curry

Master Of Buffets

Difficulty

Description

Traditional Japanese chicken curry.

B.P.M.

10 minutes preparation
50 minutes cooking

Ingredients

2 onions
1 potato
1 carrot
6⅔ oz jar of katsu curry paste
2 tablespoons olive oil
1⅛ cups basmati rice
1 large egg
2 cups panko bread crumbs
4 chicken breasts
⅓ cup rice flour
⅔ cup vegetable oil
4 teaspoons fukujinzuke (Japanese pickle), to serve

Mains

Method

1. Peel and dice 1 onion. Peel the potato and carrot and cut them into large chunks.

2. Bring 1¾ cups water to a boil in a saucepan.

3. Add the chopped onion, carrot, and potato to the pan. Reduce to a simmer, and cook for 20 minutes.

4. Pour in the katsu curry paste and stir. Simmer for an additional 10 minutes. While the curry is simmering, prepare the chicken and the rice.

5. Peel and dice the other onion. Heat the olive oil in a second saucepan over high heat. Add the diced onion and cook for 2 minutes.

6. Add the rice to the second saucepan and stir to coat the rice in the oil. Boil a kettle full of water (approx. 2½ cups), then add it to the second saucepan. Reduce the heat to a simmer, cover with a lid and do not stir the rice again. Leave to cook for 8 minutes, then remove from the heat. Remove the curry sauce from the heat.

7. Crack the egg into a bowl,

beat it, then set aside.

8. Put the panko bread crumbs in a bowl and and set aside.

9. Place the chicken breast in a bowl and add 4 tablespoons of the rice flour. Turn the chicken breasts in the bowl so that they are evenly coated in the flour, then pour the beaten egg over the chicken, and turn the breasts until well coated.

10. Heat the vegetable oil in a skillet over high heat for 2 minutes.

11. Take 1 chicken breast at a time, roll it in the bread crumbs, then carefully lower it into the oil using tongs. Reduce the heat, and cook for 10 minutes, then turn it to cook on both sides. Repeat with the remaining breasts.

12. Divide the rice between serving plates. Slice each chicken breast into thick strips, divide the chicken between the plates and pour over the curry sauce.

13. Garnish each plate with 1 teaspoon of the fukujinzuke.

Ramenstein

Du Hast Pork

Mains

Difficulty

Description

Japanese pork ramen.

B.P.M.

20 minutes preparation
3 hours 50 minutes cooking

Ingredients

1 large leek
1 carrot
3 onions
3½-inch piece of fresh ginger
8 chicken wings
6 garlic cloves
2 tablespoons olive oil
2¼ lb pork shoulder
2 green chilies
1 cup dried shiitake mushrooms
2 teaspoons pumpkin pie spice
⅓ cup soy sauce
2 tablespoons rice wine
6 scallions
5½ oz bamboo shoots
2 tablespoons rice wine vinegar
4 large eggs
10½ oz ramen noodles
7 oz collard greens

Method

For the broth:
1. Preheat the oven to 400°F.
2. Cut the carrot, onions, and leek into chunks. Peel and grate 3 inches of the ginger.
3. Place the chicken wings, carrot, leek, onions, whole garlic cloves, and grated ginger in an ovenproof baking dish. Drizzle with the oil, and roast for 40 minutes.
4. Once cooked, transfer the contents of the dish to a large saucepan and add 3 quarts + ¾ cup of water.
5. Cut the fat off the pork, and finely slice the chilies. Add the pork and pork fat to the pan with the mushrooms, pumpkin pie spice and chilies.
6. Bring to a boil, then reduce the heat and simmer for 2 hours with the lid on.
7. Remove the pork meat and set aside. Discard the pork fat. Let the liquid simmer for an additional hour with the lid off.
8. Pass the broth through a colander set over a large heatproof bowl—discard the solids in the colander.

For the seasoning:
1. Peel and grate the rest of the ginger into a bowl.
2. Add the soy sauce and rice wine and stir to combine.
Making the ramen:
1. Dice the scallions and place them in a bowl. Add the bamboo shoots and rice wine vinegar.
2. Warm the broth in a saucepan over low heat.
3. Cook the eggs in a separate pan of water for 6 minutes, then peel off the shell and halve each egg.
4. Cook the ramen noodles in a saucepan of boiling water for 2–3 minutes. Shred the collard greens, add them to the pan and cook for a minute, then drain through a colander.
5. Chop the pork into thin chunks and place in serving bowls. Add the scallion/bamboo shoots and the noodles/collard greens.
6. Pour the broth over each bowl, and stir in the seasoning mixture. Add 2 egg halves to each serving.

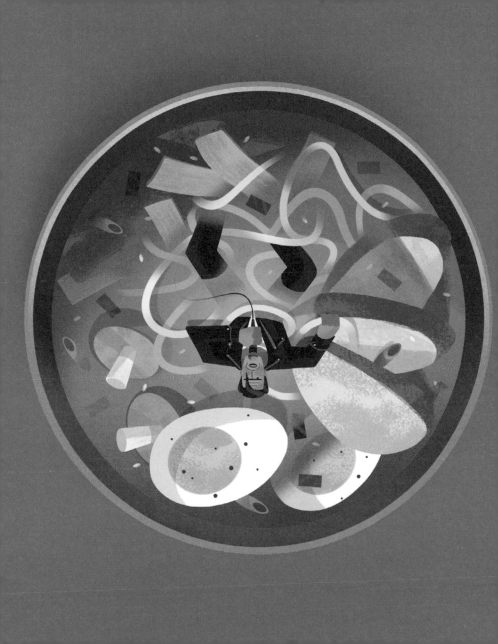

Smoked Haddock on the Water
with Deep Purple Sprouting Broccoli

Mains

Difficulty

Description

Milk-poached smoked
haddock served with steamed
purple sprouting broccoli.

B.P.M.

10 minutes preparation
15 minutes cooking

Ingredients

1 onion
4 garlic cloves
2½ cups 2% milk
7 oz purple sprouting
broccoli
4 smoked haddock fillets
A handful of flat-leaf parsley
2 tablespoons (¼ stick)
butter
Freshly ground black pepper

Method

1. Peel and dice the onion and garlic.
2. Pour the milk into a deep-sided skillet, and add the
flat-leaf parsley to the milk.
3. Add the diced onion and garlic to the milk, and season with
black pepper.
4. Place the skillet over the heat, but be careful not to boil the
milk (if it starts to bubble, reduce the heat).
5. Boil a kettle full of water, fill a separate pan below a steamer,
and place over the heat.
6. Add the smoked haddock to the milk in the skillet, and leave
it to simmer for 10 minutes.
7. Place the broccoli in the steamer, and let it steam for about
8 minutes.
8. Transfer the fish from the milk to serving plates, then drizzle
over a little of the milk sauce.
9. Add the steamed broccoli to the plate, top with a knob of
butter to melt over it, and serve.

Ladle of Filth

Tortured Bowl Asylum

Mains

Difficulty

Description

Squid ink-drenched seafood
and chorizo paella.

B.P.M.

10 minutes preparation
25 minutes cooking

Ingredients

1 red onion
2 garlic cloves
3 tablespoons olive oil
1 pot of fish stock (approx.
1 oz)
2 x ½ oz (4g) sachets
of squid ink
Heaping 1¼ cups Spanish
paella rice
1¼ cups frozen peas
A ring of chorizo
(approx. 8 oz)
7 oz raw shelled shrimp
12 oz cleaned squid
A pinch of salt
Freshly ground black pepper

Method

1. Peel and finely slice the
onion and garlic.
2. Heat 2 tablespoons of the
olive oil in a large saucepan
over high heat, add the onion,
and cook for 3 minutes.
3. Add the garlic, reduce
the heat, and cook for an
additional 2 minutes.
4. While the onion and garlic
are cooking, boil 2½ cups of
water in a kettle, then mix in a
heatproof measuring cup with
the fish stock.
5. Once the stock is mixed in,
add the squid ink to the cup
and stir thoroughly (the liquid
should turn black).
6. Tip the paella rice into the
saucepan with the garlic and
onion, and cook over low
heat, stirring, for 2 minutes.
7. Pour in the inky stock, then
turn up the heat so the liquid
bubbles. Add the frozen peas
to the pan, then turn the heat
down to low and cook for
around 12 minutes. If the paella
looks dry, add more water
(2 tablespoons at a time).
8. While the paella rice is
simmering, slice the chorizo

ring into thin discs. Heat the
remaining tablespoon of oil in
a skillet, and fry the chorizo
for 5 minutes, then set aside.
9. Add the shrimp to the
same skillet you cooked the
chorizo in, and fry them in
the chorizo-flavored oil for 5
minutes until they turn pink,
then remove and set aside.
Leave the skillet on the heat.
10. Finally slice the squid
(slice the body into rings and
keep any tentacles whole),
then tip the squid into the
skillet which was used for
the chorizo and shrimp. The
squid will shrivel quickly.
Cook for 2 minutes, then tip
the squid into the paella.
11. Turn up the heat under the
paella saucepan to medium,
then mix in the shrimp
and the chorizo and stir
thoroughly. Leave to simmer
for an additional 2 minutes.
12. Use a ladle to share the
paella between the bowls,
and season with the salt and
pepper to taste.

Primal Bream

Breamadelica

Mains

Difficulty

Description
Simple garlic- and lemon-fried
sea bream with sweet potato
wedges and cherry tomatoes.

B.P.M.
5 minutes preparation
20 minutes cooking

Ingredients
2 sweet potatoes
5 tablespoons olive oil
4 sea bream fillets
(or 2 whole bream, filleted)*
2 lemons
5 garlic cloves
1 teaspoon ground cumin
1 teaspoon smoked hot
paprika
12–16 cherry tomatoes
A pinch of salt
Freshly ground black pepper

Method
1. Preheat the oven to 400°F.
2. Peel the sweet potatoes,
cut them into wedges, and
place the wedges on a
baking sheet. Toss with 3
tablespoons of the oil, and
season with the salt and
pepper to taste.
3. Place in the center of the
oven, and cook for around
20 minutes, turning once
using tongs. While the sweet
potato is cooking, prepare
the bream.
4. Lay the fillets skin-side
down on a clean plate.
5. Cut the lemons in half
and squeeze the juices over
your bream fillets—half a
lemon per fillet. Set aside
the squeezed lemon halves.
6. Peel and dice the garlic,
and put it in a skillet with the
discarded squeezed lemon
halves, then drizzle with the
remaining oil.
7. Sprinkle the ground cumin
and paprika over the flesh
side of the fillets.
8. Cut the cherry tomatoes
into quarters and set them
aside on a plate.

9. Place the skillet containing
the oil, garlic, and lemon
halves over the heat, and
once the pan is hot,
add the bream fillets skin-
side down.
10. After 3 minutes, carefully
flip the fish over, and cook
for up to 10 minutes, until the
fish begins to lightly brown
and is cooked through. Once
the fish is cooked, remove
the fillets from the pan.
11. Remove the sweet potato
wedges from the oven and
transfer to a plate.
12. Serve the fish on plates
with the sweet potato
wedges, drizzling the fish
with any cooking juices from
the skillet.

*See Advanced Methods
p86 for filleting a fish. If
sea bream is not available,
substitute sea bass or red
snapper fillets.

Def Sheppard

When Lamb & Mash Collide

Mains

Difficulty

4

Description

Traditional shepherd's pie.

B.P.M.

15 minutes preparation
1 hour 10 minutes cooking

Ingredients

2 lb floury potatoes, such as
Yukon Gold
1 red onion
14 oz carrots
1 tablespoon sunflower oil
18 oz lean ground lamb
1 tablespoon tomato paste
1 pot of meat stock (approx.
1 oz)
3½ oz (scant 1 stick) butter
A pinch of salt

Method

1. Fill a large saucepan with 2½ cups of water. Peel the potatoes, cut them into small chunks, and add them to the pan of water. Set aside.
2. Peel and dice the red onion. Peel and cut the carrots into small chunks.
3. Heat the sunflower oil in a second saucepan. Add the carrots and onion, and fry for 2 minutes.
4. Add the lamb to the second saucepan, and cook for 8 minutes, stirring to break up any lumps of meat.
5. Add the tomato paste, and cook for an additional 4 minutes.
6. While the lamb is cooking, boil 1¼ cups of water in a kettle, then mix in a measuring cup with the meat stock. Pour this into the saucepan with the lamb, and stir thoroughly before reducing the heat. Leave to simmer for 25 minutes.
7. While the mixture is simmering, preheat the oven to 350°F.
8. Place the first saucepan containing the potatoes over high heat, and bring to a boil, then reduce the heat and simmer for 12 minutes.
9. Remove the saucepan from the heat, and drain the potatoes through a colander. Add the butter to the empty saucepan, and place it back over low heat, melt the butter in the saucepan, then add the potatoes. Add a pinch of salt, and mash the potatoes. Remove from the heat and set aside.
10. Place an ovenproof baking dish on a work surface and tip in the cooked ground lamb and vegetables, spreading it evenly across the dish.
11. Spread the mashed potato over the top of the lamb mixture. Use a fork to smooth out the potato, leaving textured lines on the surface.
12. Place the dish in the center of the oven, and bake for 30 minutes, or until the top is golden and bubbling, then serve.

Limp Brisket

Keep Rollin', Rollin', Rollin' (in spices)

Mains

Difficulty

Description
Rolled beef brisket.

B.P.M.
10 minutes preparation
3 hours 40 minutes cooking

Ingredients
2 packages of fajita
seasoning (2½ oz)*
2¼ lb beef brisket
(boned and rolled)
2 red onions
1 pot of beef stock (approx.
1oz)

Notes
Most butchers can bone and
roll the brisket for you.

Method
1. Preheat the oven to
350°F.
2. Lay the brisket out in a
casserole dish, and coat
it with 1 package of fajita
seasoning (1¼ oz), then rub it
into all sides of the meat.
3. Place the casserole dish,
uncovered, in the oven and
bake for 30 minutes. While
the brisket is cooking, empty
the second fajita package
onto a large plate and set
aside.
4. Once the brisket has
cooked, remove the dish from
the oven. Skewer the meat
with 2 forks and roll it in the
second package of seasoning
(keeping any remaining
spices for later). Return to the
casserole dish and cook in
the oven for an additional 30
minutes. While the brisket is
cooking, peel the onions and
cut them into quarters.
5. Place a saucepan over
medium heat, and pour in 2¾
cups of water. Add the stock
and onion quarters. Bring
this mixture to a simmer, then
reduce the heat, and cover

the saucepan.
6. After the brisket has
cooked, remove the casserole
dish from the oven. Skewer
the meat with 2 forks and roll
it in the remaining seasoning.
7. Pour the contents of the
saucepan into the casserole
dish. Add any remaining
seasoning from the plate,
and place the meat in the
center of the dish. Cover the
casserole dish with a lid, and
return to the oven.
8. Reduce the oven
temperature to 300°F and
cook for 2 hours 30 minutes.
9. Once the brisket is cooked,
remove the casserole dish
from the oven. Remove the
meat from the dish and place
on a plate. Cover with foil and
leave to rest for 10 minutes.
10. To serve, slice the beef
thinly across the grain. Pour
the juices and onions from
the casserole dish over the
meat as you serve it.

*See Advanced Methods p86
to make your own spicy
fajita seasoning.

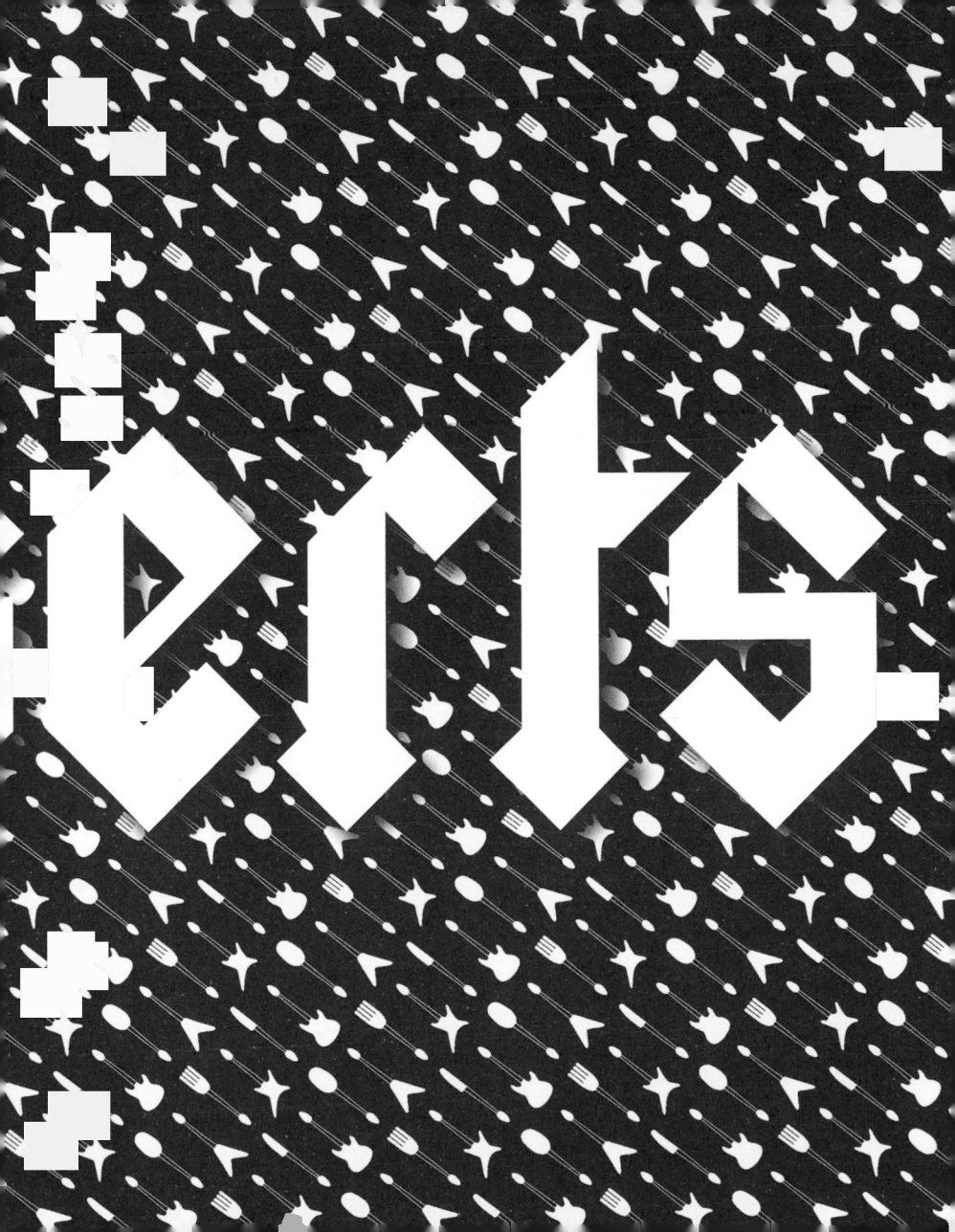

Iron Raisin

Rum To The Hills

Desserts

Difficulty

Description

Crispy rum and raisin cakes.

B.P.M.

At least 1 hour preparation (ideally soak the raisins the night before)
30 minutes baking

Ingredients

¾ cup raisins
⅓ cup white rum,
plus extra for drizzling
3½ oz (scant 1 stick) butter
⅓ cup soft light brown sugar
1 egg
1 cup whole-wheat bread crust (or bread crumbs)
Heaping ¼ cup self-rising flour
½ teaspoon ground cinnamon
4 scoops of vanilla ice cream, to serve (optional)

Method

1. Put the raisins in a mixing bowl, add the rum, and leave them to soak overnight (if you don't have time, you can leave them for an hour, but it is best if the rum has time to be absorbed by the fruit).

2. Preheat the oven to 350°F.

3. Grease 4 holes of a muffin pan with half of the butter.

4. In a mixing bowl combine the remaining butter with the brown sugar.

5. Crack the egg into the bowl and mix well.

6. Put the whole-wheat bread crust into a food processor and blend into bread crumbs (if you're using pre-made bread crumbs you don't need to blend them). Add this to the bowl and mix thoroughly.

7. Add the self-rising flour and the ground cinnamon.

8. Tip in the rum-soaked raisins and any remaining soaking liquid. Mix thoroughly.

9. Spoon out the mixture into the greased molds in the muffin pan (this mixture should make 4 rum and raisin cakes).

10. Place in the oven to bake for 30 minutes (or until they begin to brown and crisp).

11. Remove the pan from the oven, and transfer the cakes from the muffin pan to a cooling rack. Serve warm with a scoop of vanilla ice cream, if liked, and drizzle a teaspoonful of rum over each serving.

Slayer Cake

Angel Of Death Cake

Desserts

Difficulty

Description

A three-tiered angel cake.

B.P.M.

45 minutes preparation
35 minutes baking

Ingredients

19½ oz (scant 5 sticks) unsalted butter
1 lb superfine sugar
5 large eggs
1 tablespoon vanilla extract
1 lb (scant 3½ cups) all-purpose flour
2 teaspoons baking powder
Generous 1¼ cups sour cream
Heaping ⅓ cup cocoa powder
⅓ cup chocolate chips
2⅛ cups confectioners' sugar
3 oz dark chocolate, chopped
A jar of strawberry jam
10 raspberries
25–30 blueberries

Method

1. Grease 3 x 9-inch cake pans with 1¾ oz (a scant ½ stick) of the butter, then line with parchment paper.
2. Preheat the oven to 375°F.
3. Place the superfine sugar and 13¾ oz (scant 3½ sticks) of the butter in a bowl and whisk until creamy.
4. Whisk in the eggs one by one until combined, then add 2 teaspoons of vanilla extract.
5. Sift 1¾ cups of the flour with the baking powder, and fold it into the mixture with half of the sour cream.
6. Sift in the rest of the flour (1¾ cups) and stir in the rest of the sour cream.
7. Divide the mixture between three bowls and add ingredients as follows:
Bowl 1—fold in cocoa powder.
Bowl 2—mix in chocolate chips.
Bowl 3—leave as is.
8. Transfer the 3 mixtures into the pans and bake in the oven for 35 minutes.
9. Leave to cool for 5 minutes, then transfer the cakes from their pans to a cooling rack.
10. In a bowl mix the remaining 4oz (1 stick) butter with the confectioners' sugar and remaining vanilla extract.
11. Melt the chocolate in a bowl over a pan of simmering water, then remove from the heat and cool for 2 minutes.
12. Mix the melted chocolate into the confectioners' sugar and butter mixture.
13. Spread jam across the top of the chocolate sponge.
14. Spread chocolate icing on the underside of the chocolate chip sponge.
15. Lift the chocolate chip cake and place it, icing-side down on the jam-covered chocolate layer.
16. Spread jam on top of the chocolate chip sponge.
17. Spread chocolate icing on the underside of the plain sponge, then place it on top of the jam-covered chocolate chip cake so you have 3 layers.
18. Spread the rest of the chocolate icing on the top and sides of the cake, smoothing until fully covered.
19. Decorate with the berries.

The Rolling Scones

If You Try Sometimes, You Get What You Knead

Desserts

Difficulty

Description

Traditional British scones with brown sugar and currants

B.P.M.

15 minutes preparation
15 minutes baking

Ingredients

2 tablespoons all-purpose flour, for dusting
2oz (½ stick) unsalted butter
1¾ cups self-rising flour
A pinch of salt
⅓ cup turbinado sugar
Scant ¼ cup golden raisins
¾ cup milk
Butter, cream, and strawberry jam, to serve

Method

1. Preheat the oven to 425°F.
2. Line 2 baking sheets with parchment paper, then dust ½ tablespoon of all-purpose flour over each of the lined sheets.
3. Cube the butter, and put it in a large mixing bowl with the self-rising flour and salt.
4. Using your fingertips, mix the self-rising flour and salt into the butter.
5. Add 2½ tablespoons of the sugar and all the golden raisins to the bowl, and stir the mixture together.
6. Pour ⅔ cup of the milk into the bowl and stir until the mixture forms a soft dough.
7. Dust a clean work surface with the rest of the all-purpose flour. Transfer the dough to the work surface and knead it lightly.
8. Flatten out the kneaded dough and press it down into a sheet that is about ¾ inch thick.
9. Use a 2-inch cookie cutter to cut out discs of dough, and lay them on the lined and floured baking sheets. (If you do not have a cookie cutter, use a small cup as a template, and cut around it).
10. Collect the offcuts, and lightly knead again, repeating the process until all the dough has been cut into small discs. The mixture makes approx. 10 scones.
11. Using a pastry brush, glaze the tops of the scones with the remaining milk.
12. Sprinkle the remaining 2½ tablespoons of turbinado sugar over the scones.
13. Place the baking sheets with the scones in the oven, and bake for 15 minutes until golden brown.
14. Remove from the oven, and transfer the scones to a cooling rack.
15. For best results, serve the scones warm, with butter, cream, and jam to taste.

Smashing Pumpkin Pie

Flava Adore

Desserts

Difficulty

(dial showing 7)

Description

Classic pumpkin pie.

B.P.M.

20 minutes preparation
(plus cooling)
1 hour 15 minutes baking

Ingredients

1 tablespoon all-purpose
flour
12 oz ready-made pie dough*
2 large eggs
1 x 15oz can puréed pumpkin
1 x 14oz can sweetened
condensed milk
1 teaspoon ground cinnamon
½ teaspoon ground cloves
1 teaspoon ground ginger
½ teaspoon ground nutmeg
or
1 tablespoon pumpkin pie
spice
A pinch of salt
Whipping cream (as much as
you wish)

Method

1. Lightly dust a clean work surface with the flour. Lay out the pie dough, and roll it until it is around ¼ inch thick.
2. Line a 9-inch tart pan with the pie dough, and place in the fridge for 10 minutes.
3. Preheat your oven to 350°F.
4. Take the tart pan out of the fridge, and line with parchment paper, then fill with baking beans.
5. Place the tart pan on the middle shelf of the oven and bake for 15 minutes.
6. Remove the baking beans and parchment paper, then return the tart pan to the oven and bake for an additional 10 minutes.
7. Remove the tart pan from the oven and set aside.
8. Increase the oven temperature to 450°F.
9. Crack the eggs into a mixing bowl, then add the puréed pumpkin, condensed milk, ground cinnamon, ground cloves, ground ginger, ground nutmeg (or pumpkin pie spice) and salt. Whisk the ingredients until even in color and well combined.
10. Pour the mixture into the tart case, and gently tap the edges of the tart pan to settle the mixture.
11. Place the tart on the middle shelf of the oven and bake for 10 minutes.
12. Reduce the oven temperature to 350°F, and bake for an additional 50 minutes.
13. Take the pie out of the oven, and set aside to cool for 10 minutes. Transfer the pie to the fridge, and allow to cool for at least another 15 minutes.
14. While the pie is cooling, pour some whipping cream into a bowl and whisk vigorously by hand or with an electric whisk until thick.
15. Carefully remove the pumpkin pie from the pan. Serve a slice of pie with a dollop of the whipping cream.

*See Advanced Methods p87 to make pie dough.

Nirvana Split

Smells Like Teen Spirit

Desserts

Difficulty

Description

Baked peach and banana split with a whiskey twist.

B.P.M.

40 minutes preparation
1 hour 10 minutes cooking

Ingredients

4 peaches
3 tablespoons Scotch whiskey
2 limes
Generous ½ cup date nectar or golden syrup
3½ oz dark chocolate
4 bananas
4 scoops of ice cream
Aerosol whipped cream

Notes

For best results, use a whiskey aged at least 12 years.

Method

1. Cut the peaches in half and remove the pits.
2. Place the peach halves in an ovenproof baking dish, and drizzle over the whiskey. Cut the limes in half, and squeeze the juice from each half over the peaches. Place in the fridge, and leave the peaches to soak for 30 minutes.
3. Preheat the oven to 425°F.
4. Take the dish out of the fridge, and cover the peaches with the date nectar or golden syrup.
5. Place in the oven and cook for 1 hour.
6. While the peaches are baking, blitz the chocolate in the food processor until finely ground (if you don't have a food processor, use a grater or finely chop the chocolate with a knife).
7. Once cooked, remove the peaches from the oven, and spoon them into a mixing bowl.
8. Tip the ground chocolate over the peaches and gently turn the mixture, being careful not to break the peaches.
9. Slice the 4 bananas in half lengthwise, and place each pair of the banana halves in a bowl. Place 2 peach halves on top of each serving.
10. Divide the remaining nectar and chocolate mix between each bowl, pouring it over the banana and peaches.
11. Before serving, add a scoop of ice cream to each bowl, and aerosol whipped cream to your taste.

Spinal Tapioca

These Go To Gas Mark 11

Desserts

Difficulty

Description

Creamy tapioca pudding with mini "Stonehenge" cookies.

B.P.M.

4 hours preparation
20 minutes cooking

Ingredients

3 large eggs
3 cups whole milk
1⅛ cups tapioca
A pinch of salt
⅞ cup granulated sugar
4 teaspoons vanilla extract
9 oz (1¼ sticks) butter
¾ cup superfine sugar
2¼ cups all-purpose flour
(plus an extra tablespoon
for dusting)

Method

For the tapioca:
1. Break 2 of the eggs into a mixing bowl and beat together, then set aside.
2. Combine the milk, tapioca, salt, and granulated sugar in a saucepan.
3. Place the saucepan over high heat, and stir the mixture for 3 minutes.
4. Reduce the heat to low, and stir for an another 5 minutes.
5. Remove the saucepan from the heat, and continue to stir the mixture. Add the beaten egg, a tablespoon at a time, stirring continuously, then stir for another minute.
6. Place the saucepan back over medium heat, and stir continuously for 90 seconds.
7. Remove the saucepan from the heat for a final time, and stir in half the vanilla extract.
8. Divide the mixture between 4 serving glasses, and leave to cool for 30 minutes, then place in the fridge and chill for 3 hours. While the spinal tapioca is chilling, you can make the "Stonehenges" as described on the right.

For the 'Stonehenge' cookies:
1. Turn your oven to 500°F (or its highest setting).
2. Combine the butter and superfine sugar in a bowl until light and fluffy.
3. Yolk the remaining egg*, then add the yolk and the remaining vanilla extract to the bowl. Stir for 1 minute. Add the flour to the mixture and stir for 4 minutes.
5. Line a baking sheet with parchment paper.
6. Dust a work surface with the tablespoon of flour and lay out the cookie dough.
7. Roll out the dough until it is ¼ inch thick.
8. Cut it into 12 rectangles about 1⅓ inches wide by 4 inches long, and lay them out on the baking sheet.
9. Place the sheet in the oven and bake for 10 minutes.
10. Transfer the cookies to a cooling rack to harden.
11. Construct a "Stonehenge" from 3 cookies per bowl, and serve on top of the tapioca.

*See Advanced Methods p85.

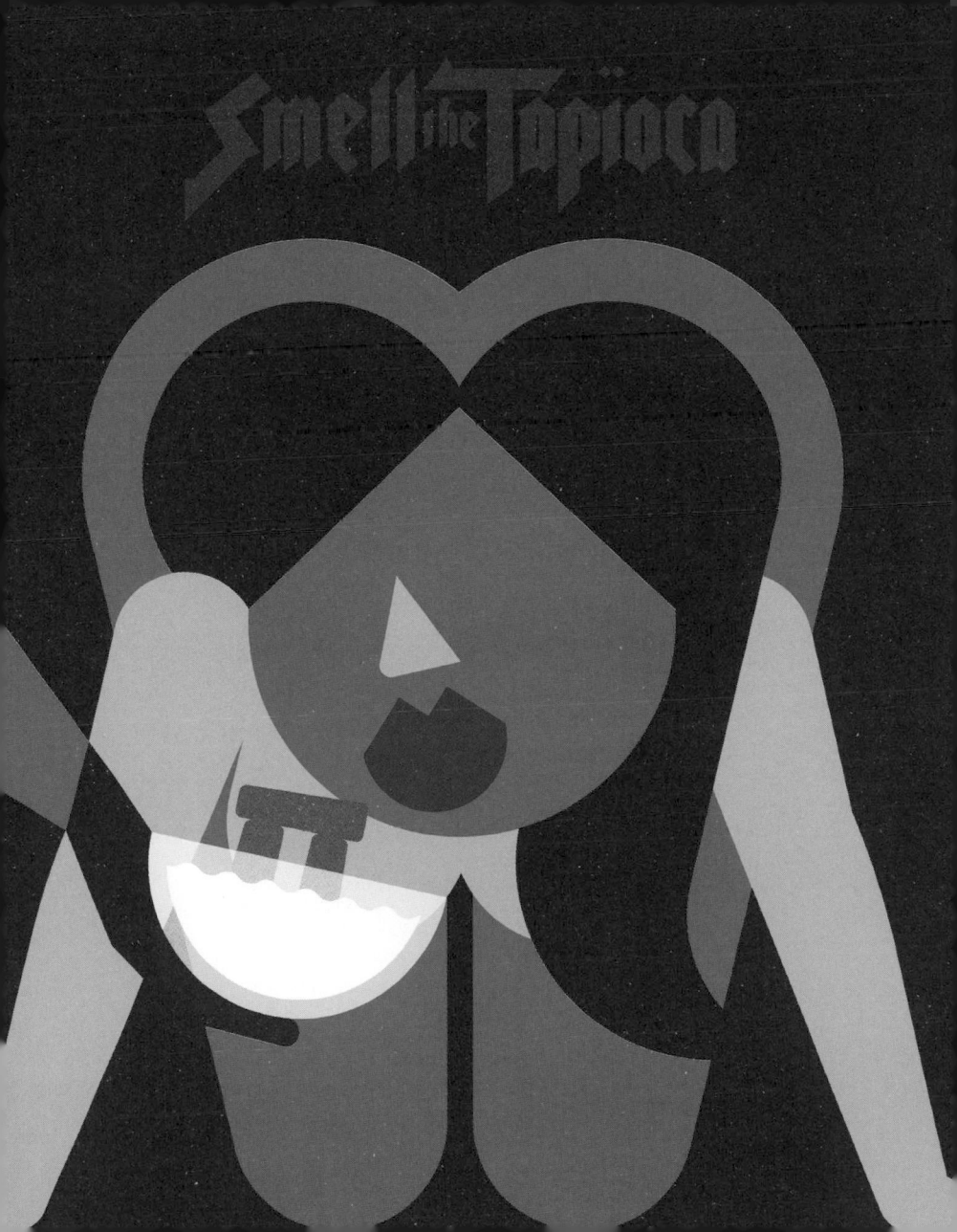

Dire Dates

Sultanas Of Swing

Desserts

Difficulty

Description

Sticky, boozy date and sultana (golden raisin) molasses cake.

B.P.M.

20 minutes preparation
45 minutes baking

Ingredients

7 oz pitted dates
²⁄₃ cup Cointreau or brandy
9½ oz (approx. 2½ sticks) butter
¾ cup golden raisins
Scant 1½ cups dark brown sugar
3 tablespoons molasses
2⅛ cups all-purpose flour
¾ teaspoon baking soda
1 teaspoon baking powder
2 teaspoons ground ginger
A pinch of salt
3 large eggs
⅞ cup orange juice
3 oranges
1¼ cups heavy cream

Method

For the cake:

1. Roughly chop the dates, then put them in a saucepan and add 7 tablespoons of the Cointreau or brandy.

2. Add the raisins, and warm gently over low heat for 5 minutes, then set aside.

3. Preheat the oven to 350°F.

4. Beat 4oz (1 stick) of the butter in a bowl with a heaping ½ cup of the sugar.

5. Add the molasses and beat it into the mixture. Beat well for 3–4 minutes until almost fluffy.

6. In a separate mixing bowl, combine the flour with the baking soda, baking powder, ground ginger, and salt, and set aside.

7. Crack the eggs and beat them into the molasses mixture, one at a time, sifting in about ⅛ of the flour mixture as you go, and stir thoroughly. Once all the eggs are mixed in, sift in the rest of the flour mixture.

8. Heat the orange juice in the microwave for 30 seconds (or on the stovetop in a separate saucepan) until lukewarm, then pour the juice into the cake mixture and stir.

9. Spoon in the alcohol-soaked fruit and mix, then grate the zest of 2 of the oranges into the mixture and stir.

10. Grease the base of an ovenproof baking dish with 1¾oz (½ stick) of the butter, then line the base with parchment paper.

11. Spoon in the cake mixture, then place in the oven, and bake for 45 minutes. While it is baking, prepare the sauce.

For the sauce:

1. Put the remaining butter and dark brown sugar in a pan, and place over low heat to melt, stirring thoroughly.

2. Whisk in the heavy cream, then increase the heat until the sauce begins to bubble. While it is cooking, grate in the zest of the remaining orange and stir thoroughly.

3. Once it is well mixed and warm, add the rest of the Cointreau or brandy and stir.

4. Serve by pouring the sauce over the cake.

Sepultempura Fried Ice Cream

Scoops Of Doom

Desserts

Difficulty

10

Description

Tempura fried ice cream.

B.P.M.

6 hours 10 minutes
preparation (at least)
12 minutes cooking

Ingredients

8 slices of brown bread
3 tablespoons honey
8 scoops of vanilla ice cream
(or flavor of choice)
Ice cubes (approx. 20 cubes)
²/₃ cup all-purpose flour
A pinch of salt
½ teaspoon granulated sugar
⁷/₈ cup chilled sparkling water
Sunflower oil (enough to fill
a deep-fat fryer)

Method

1. Slice the crusts off the bread and lay the slices out on a clean work surface.
2. Spread a thin layer of honey over the top of each slice of bread.
3. Drop a round scoop of ice cream (roughly 1¼ inches in diameter) in the center of the bread.
4. Wrap the bread slices around the ice cream balls, cut away any excess bread, and patch any gaps with the offcuts (it is important that no ice cream is exposed). Repeat this until you have 8 ice cream and bread balls.
5. Tightly wrap each ball in plastic wrap, twisting the ends of the wrap to form a round ball. Place the wrapped balls in the freezer, and leave to freeze for at least 6 hours (the longer they are frozen the better).
6. When ready to serve, heat the deep-fat fryer to its maximum setting (the oil should be very hot).
7. Place several sheets of paper towels on a plate,

ready to soak up any excess oil from the cooked tempura.
8. Unwrap the plastic wrap around the frozen balls.
9. Half-fill a large bowl with ice cubes, and position a smaller bowl inside it (so that the smaller bowl is surrounded by ice).
10. Add the flour, salt, and sugar to the smaller bowl.
11. Whisk the sparkling water into the mixture for 1 minute (do not over-whisk as this will cause the batter to over-thicken, and absorb too much oil during cooking).
12. Using tongs, dip one frozen ball into the batter mix in the smaller bowl, coat it in the batter, let the excess drip off, then drop it carefully into the hot oil in the deep-fat fryer. Fry for 90 seconds, then transfer to the paper towels to drain the excess oil. Repeat this process until all 8 balls have been fried.
13. Serve the balls immediately, before the ice cream has a chance to melt.

Judas Peach

Ram It Down

Desserts

Difficulty

Description

A classic crisp and oaty peach crumble.

B.P.M.

10 minutes preparation
50 minutes baking

Ingredients

5 ripe peaches
½ lemon
3–4 tablespoons turbinado sugar
1⅓ cups all-purpose flour
3½oz (scant 1 stick) unsalted butter
A pinch of salt
1 tablespoon rolled oats

Method

1. Preheat the oven to 375°F.
2. Skin the peaches, then cut them into thin wedges and remove the pits.
3. Place the peach wedges in a small ovenproof dish, so they cover the base.
4. Grate the zest of the ½ lemon and mix it in a bowl with the juice of the ½ lemon, then add a tablespoon of the turbinado sugar and stir thoroughly.
5. Pour the lemon and sugar mixture over the peaches.
6. Place the flour, 2 tablespoons of the turbinado sugar, and all the butter in a food processor with the salt (if you don't have a food processor, you can mix it all thoroughly in a bowl with your fingertips).
7. Sprinkle the crumble mix over the peaches, and press it down with a fork to ensure that the peaches are thoroughly covered.
8. Sprinkle the rolled oats over the crumble (you can also add another tablespoon of sugar to taste).
9. Bake the crumble in the oven for 50 minutes.
10. Remove from the oven, and leave to cool for 5 minutes before serving.

Whitesnaked Alaska

Here I Go Meringue On My Own

Difficulty

Description

A true retro classic with ice cream on a bed of sponge cake and Italian meringue.

B.P.M.

6 hours 30 minutes preparation (at least)
15 minutes cooking

Ingredients

Vanilla ice cream (enough to fill your freezable bowl)
3 large eggs*
Scant 1 cup granulated sugar
Syrup sponge cake (enough to make a circular layer the same diameter as your freezable bowl)*

Notes

Make sure the saucepan you heat the sugar in is very clean —any residue in the pan will ruin the sugar syrup.

Method

1. Place a dome-shaped freezable bowl (no wider than 4 inches) upside down on top of a piece of parchment paper. Use this as a guide to create a circular stencil the same diameter as the bowl.
2. Line the freezable bowl with plastic wrap. Pack the lined bowl with ice cream, pushing the ice cream down. Flatten the top of the ice cream, then cover the bowl with another sheet of plastic wrap. Place this in the freezer for at least 6 hours.
3. Yolk the eggs*, then pour the whites into a spotlessly clean large bowl. (Discard the yolks, or use in another recipe.) Whisk the whites until they form soft peaks.
4. Place a saucepan over medium heat, and add the sugar and 7 tablespoons water. Heat for 3 minutes, and stir, until it turns light brown.
5. Set the electric whisk on its lowest setting, and continually whisk the egg whites, while you very slowly pour the hot sugar syrup down the side of

the bowl (don't add the syrup too quickly, as it will scald and deflate the egg whites). This should take 2 minutes.
6. Turn the electric whisk to its highest setting, and whisk for 4–6 minutes, until the meringue is thick and glossy.
7. Cut the syrup sponge cake into a 2-inch thick layer.
8. Using the parchment paper stencil as a guide, cut a disc the same diameter as the bowl from the syrup sponge, and place the disc on a plate.
9. Take the ice cream out of the freezer, and remove the top layer of plastic wrap. Place the flat side of the ice cream on top of the cake disc. This will form a dome of ice cream on top of the cake. Remove the bowl and the rest of the plastic wrap.
10. Spread the meringue mixture over the ice cream.
11. Just before serving, use a blow torch to quickly brown the outside of the meringue.

*See Advanced Methods p85 to yolk an egg, and p87 to make your own syrup sponge cake.

Desserts

Supporting Acts

Bruce's Spring Greens

Description
A zesty green walnut salad.

B.P.M.
10 minutes preparation/cooking

Ingredients
2 sweetheart lettage cabbages
1 lemon
1 garlic clove
⅓ cup walnuts
1 tablespoon butter

Supporting
Primal Bream, Limp Brisket

Method
1. Slice the sweetheart lettage into thin strips, and discard the ends. Cut the lemon in half, and squeeze the juice into a bowl.
2. Dice the garlic, and add it to the bowl with the lemon juice.
3. Chop the walnuts, add them to the bowl with the garlic, and mix.
4. Boil a kettle full of water.
5. Place the sweetheart lettage in the saucepan over the heat, add the boiled water, and cook for 3 minutes.
6. Drain through a colander, and set aside.
7. Place a skillet over the heat. Add the butter, drained sweetheart lettage, lemon, garlic, and walnuts, and cook for 2–3 minutes.
8. Remove from the heat and serve—pouring over any juices.

Bruce's Spring Greens illustration by Alice Moloney
www.alicemoloney.com

Korn on the Cob

Description
Zingy, herby corn on the cob.

B.P.M.
12 minutes preparation/cooking

Ingredients
A sprig of cilantro
1 lime
4 corn cobs
1oz (¼ stick) butter

Supporting
Tex-Mex Pistols, Limp Brisket

Method
1. Finely dice the cilantro leaves and put them in a bowl.
2. Cut the lime in half and squeeze the juice of both halves into the bowl.
3. Boil a kettle full of water and pour into a saucepan, then place over the heat, add the corn, and boil for 6 minutes.
4. Remove the saucepan from the heat and drain the corn through a colander.
5. Put the butter in the saucepan, and place over low heat. Once it melts, add the cilantro and lime, and stir.
6. Roll the corn in the butter, mint, cilantro, and lime, then serve, drizzling it with the contents of the saucepan.

PoToto Roasties

Description
Deliciously crisp
roast potatoes.

B.P.M.
10 minutes preparation
40 minutes cooking

Ingredients
2¼ lb potatoes
A pinch of salt
⅓ cup olive oil
3 tablespoons polenta
2 sprigs of rosemary
Freshly ground black pepper

Supporting
Smoked Haddock on the Water

Method
1. Preheat the oven to 400°F.
2. Peel and cut the potatoes into 2-inch chunks.
3. Boil a kettle full of water, and pour the water into a saucepan. Add the potatoes and salt, and boil for 8 minutes.
4. Once boiled, remove the saucepan from the heat, drain the potatoes through a colander, and return them to the saucepan.
5. Add 3 tablespoons of the oil to a baking pan, and place in the oven for 5 minutes to get hot.
6. Sprinkle the polenta over the potatoes in the saucepan. Hold a lid over the pan, and shake it for 20 seconds to roughen the surface of the potatoes and coat them in the polenta.
7. Remove the baking pan from the oven, and place the potatoes in the hot oil. Pour over the rest of the oil. Sprinkle over the rosemary needles, and add pepper to taste.
8. Place the potatoes in the oven, and cook for 35 minutes, or until golden brown, turning them several times to ensure all sides crisp up. Remove from the oven and serve.

Bachman-Turnip Overdrive

Description
Turnip, carrot, and sage mash.

B.P.M.
5 minutes preparation
25 minutes cooking

Ingredients
4 small turnips
3 carrots
1oz (¼ stick) butter
1 teaspoon dried sage
A pinch of salt

Supporting
ZZ Chop, Limp Brisket

Method
1. Peel the turnips and carrots, and cut them into small chunks.
2. Boil a kettle full of water and pour it into a saucepan. Place the saucepan over medium heat, add the turnip and carrot, and cook for 20 minutes.
3. Remove the saucepan from the heat, and drain the turnips and carrots through a colander.
4. Put the butter in the saucepan, and place it over low heat.
5. Add the turnip and carrot, and mash with a masher or fork.
6. Sprinkle in the sage and salt, and stir thoroughly.
7. Divide evenly between the plates to serve.

Supporting Acts

Soundgarden Salad

Description
Garden salad with tarragon.

B.P.M.
5 minutes preparation

Ingredients
1 salad tomato
1 red bell pepper
1 avocado
3½ oz spinach
3½ oz arugula
2 tablespoons olive oil
1 tablespoon balsamic vinegar
1 teaspoon dried tarragon

Supporting
Tex-Mex Pistols, ZZ Chop

Method
1. Slice the tomato in half, then cut each half into quarters.
2. Halve the red pepper, remove the stalk and scrape away the pith and seeds. Cut the pepper into thin slices.
3. Cut the avocado in half and remove the pit. Using a knife, remove the skin, then dice the flesh.
4. Place the spinach and arugula in a mixing bowl. Add the tomato, pepper, and avocado. Mix the salad to ensure the ingredients are well distributed throughout the bowl.
5. Pour the oil into a cup, add the balsamic vinegar, and the tarragon, and stir thoroughly.
6. Drizzle the dressing over the salad and serve.

Andrew W. Kale

Description
Spicy kale with mushrooms.

B.P.M.
5 minutes preparation
8 minutes cooking

Ingredients
1 garlic clove
1 oz mushrooms
3½ oz chopped kale
1 teaspoon olive oil
1 teaspoon hot smoked paprika

Supporting
Primal Bream, Def Sheppard

Method
1. Peel and dice the garlic. Finely chop the mushrooms.
2. Boil a kettle full of water, then pour it into the saucepan. Place over medium heat, and add the kale. Boil for 4 minutes.
3. Heat the oil in a skillet over high heat, and add the mushrooms and garlic. Sprinkle over the paprika.
4. Remove the saucepan from the heat, and drain the kale, then add it to the garlic and mushrooms, and cook for an additional 3 minutes.
5. Spoon the contents of the skillet onto plates, and drizzle over the pan juices.

Supporting Acts

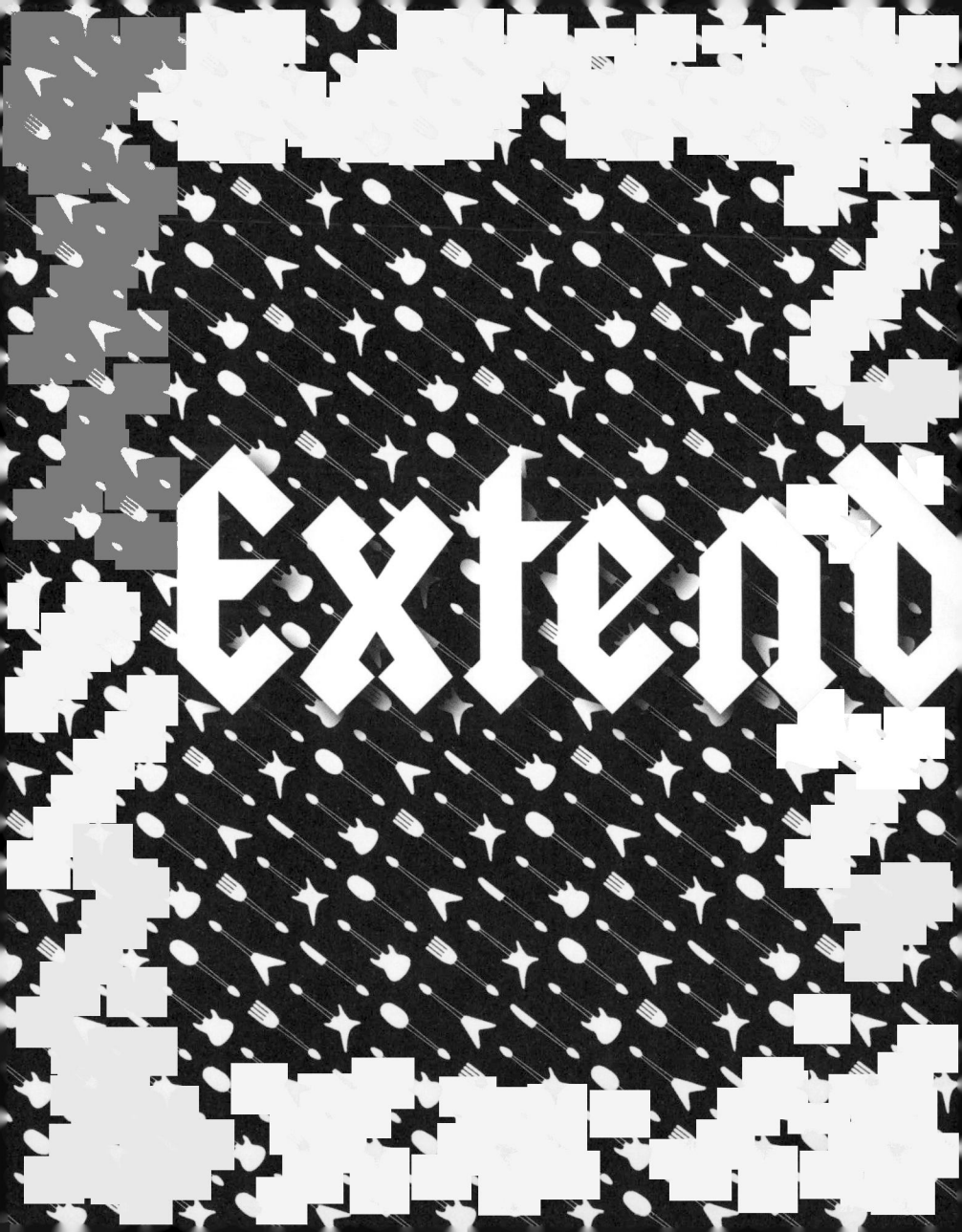

Advanced Methods

Pho Spice Mix

Ingredients
½ oz cinnamon sticks
½ oz whole cloves
½ oz whole star anise
½ oz cardamom pods
½ oz coriander seeds

Featured in
Status Pho

Method
1. Put all the ingredients in a mixing bowl.
2. Mix the ingredients thoroughly.
3. Fill a cheesecloth spice bag with the spice mix and pull the drawstring tight.

Notes
This quantity makes approx. 2½ oz spice mix, for one pot of pho. You can make a bigger batch by increasing the ingredients proportionally. Store in a jar in a cool, dark closet away from sunlight, and the spices will last around 6 months.

Pho Bone Stock

Ingredients
8 oz fresh beef bones

Featured in
Status Pho

Method
1. Preheat your oven to 425°F.
2. Put the beef bones in a baking pan, place it in the oven, and roast for 1 hour.
3. Transfer the bones to a large saucepan, and cover with 8½ cups of water. Bring to a boil, then reduce the heat to a simmer. Cover the saucepan with a lid, and leave to simmer for 1 hour.
4. Remove the saucepan from the heat, and leave the stock to cool for 30 minutes.
5. If you have a fat strainer, pour in the stock and allow the mixture to fully separate before pouring out. (Alternatively, place a clean cotton dish towel over a colander. Place the colander and dish towel over a bowl and pour the stock through to catch the fat.)

Sweet Chili Dipping Sauce

Ingredients

3 garlic cloves
2 red chilies
3 tablespoons white
wine vinegar
½ cup superfine sugar
A pinch of salt
1 tablespoon cornstarch

Featured in

The Offspring Rolls

Method

1. Peel the garlic cloves, and remove any stems from the chilies.
2. Put the garlic, chilies, vinegar, sugar, salt, and ⅔ cup water in a blender, then blitz until the mixture forms a thin purée.
3. Pour the mixture into a saucepan, and bring to a boil.
4. Reduce the heat, and allow the mixture to simmer for 4 minutes.
5. Add the cornstarch a little at a time, mixing with a whisk.
6. Remove the saucepan from the heat, and leave to cool for at least 30 minutes.
7. The sauce will keep for around 2 weeks. To store, decant it into a clean glass bottle or jar, seal, and leave in the fridge.

Yolking an Egg

Ingredients

1 egg

Featured in

Dim Sum 41
Spinal Tapioca
Whitesnaked Alaska

Method

1. Being careful not to break the yolk, crack the egg in half over a cup and tilt it so that the yolk remains in one half of the shell—some white will drop into the cup.
2. With the other half of the shell in your other hand, tilt the egg shell with the yolk in it so that most of the white pours into the cup, then allow the yolk to drop into the empty half of the egg shell.
3. Gently tip the yolk into a second cup. This will give you one cup of egg white, and the other with the yolk.

Extended Play

Spicy Fajita Seasoning

Ingredients

2 tablespoons cornstarch
2²⁄₃ tablespoons hot chili powder
1¹⁄₃ tablespoons salt
1¹⁄₃ tablespoons paprika
1¹⁄₃ tablespoons soft light brown sugar
2 teaspoons onion powder/onion granules
1 teaspoon garlic powder
2 teaspoons cayenne pepper
1 teaspoon ground cumin

Featured in

Limp Brisket, Tex-Mex Pistols

Method

1. Put all the ingredients in a mixing bowl.
2. Mix the ingredients thoroughly.

Notes

This quantity makes 3 oz of seasoning—it can be scaled up by increasing the ingredients proportionally.

Filleting a Fish

Ingredients

Fish

Featured in

Primal Bream

Method

1. If the fish has been scaled, but not yet gutted, slice open the underside of the fish with a sharp knife and remove the fish's guts using a teaspoon.
2. Cut behind the gills and the wing of the fish, then turn it over. Do the same on the other side, so the head comes loose. You can now discard the head.
3. Using the spine as your guide, slice just inside the spine from the tail to the top of the fish—open it up and pull the side it away from the bones.
4. If any of the fillet does not come loose from the bones, use the knife to release the fillet from the body.
5. Turn the fish over and repeat—giving you two fillets, and a bony central part of the fish which can be discarded.
6. Use a tweezer to pull any small bones from the fillet, being careful not to break apart the flesh. Rinse the fillets.

Pie Dough

Ingredients

3½ oz (scant 1 stick) unsalted
butter
1¾ cups all-purpose flour,
plus 1 tablespoon to dust
A pinch of salt

Featured in

Smashing Pumpkin Pie

Method

1. Cut the butter into ¾ inch cubes and set aside.
2. Sift the flour into a mixing bowl and add the butter.
3. Using your fingertips, rub the butter and flour together until
the mix resembles bread crumbs, with no lumps of butter.
4. Add the salt and 3 tablespoons of cold water. Using a
spoon, mix together to form a dough.
5. Dust the work surface with the tablespoon of flour.
6. Gently knead the dough on the floured work surface.
7. Wrap in plastic wrap and chill in the fridge until required.

Syrup Sponge Cake

Ingredients

7 oz (1¾ sticks) unsalted
butter
½ cup superfine sugar
2 large eggs
¼ cup golden syrup
1½ cups self-rising flour

Featured in

Whitesnaked Alaska

Method

1. Preheat the oven to 350°F.
2. Line a cake pan with parchment paper.
3. Place the butter and sugar in a mixing bowl, and mix together
using a fork, until it becomes soft and fluffy.
4. Beat the eggs into the butter and sugar, one at a time, then
add the golden syrup and mix.
5. Add the flour, and mix until smooth.
6. Scrape the mixture into the cake pan, level it out with a
spatula, and place in the oven for 40 minutes, or until golden
brown.
7. Remove from the oven, and set aside to cool on a wire rack.

Extended Play

Recipe Index—Appetizers

The Recipe Index is your guide to all the recipes in the book, allowing you to see at a glance the difficulty and the time it takes to make each recipe. We have also listed dietary and allergen information, as follows:

☉ Vegetarian
℗ Pescatarian
Ⓖ Gluten-free

EASIEST
Pig Floyd
1/11

HARDEST
The Offspring Rolls
9/11

QUICKEST
The Offspring Rolls
20 mins/5 mins

SLOWEST
Status Pho
15 mins/4 hours 15 mins

12
Fleetwood Mac & Cheese
Difficulty: 4/11
B.P.M.: 25 mins/25 mins
☉ ℗
by Eve Lloyd Knight
evelloydknight.co.uk

20
Captain Beeftart
Difficulty: 4/11
B.P.M.: 40 mins/30 mins

by Tom J. Newell
tomjnewell.com

22
Suzi Quatro Formaggi
Difficulty: 5/11
B.P.M.: 1 hour 25 mins/15 mins
☉ ℗
by Lynnie Zulu
lynniezulu.com

24
Slip Gnocchi
Difficulty: 6/11
B.P.M.: 15 mins/1 hour 10 mins
☉ ℗
by Ewen Farr
unfarr.com

Dark Side of the Spoon

14
Pig Floyd
Difficulty: 1/11
B.P.M.: 10 mins/25 mins

by Will Finlay
wbfinlay.tumblr.com

16
Tofu Fighters
Difficulty: 3/11
B.P.M.: 5 mins/20 mins

by Anje Jager
anjejager.com

18
Beef Patty Smith
Difficulty: 4/11
B.P.M.: 15 mins/15 mins

by Annemarieke Kloosterhof
annemariekekloosterhof.com

Extended Play

26
Status Pho
Difficulty: 6/11
B.P.M.: 15 mins/4 hours 15 mins

by Joe Sparkes
joe-sparkes.com

28
The Offspring Rolls
Difficulty: 9/11
B.P.M.: 20 mins/5 mins

by Matt Robinson
matthewrobinson.co.uk

30
Dim Sum 41
Difficulty: 7/11
B.P.M.: 30 mins/8 mins

by Joe Bichard
joebichard.com

Recipe Index—Mains

34
Tex-Mex Pistols
Difficulty: 6/11
B.P.M.: 15 mins/15 mins

by Adam Cruft
adamcruft.com

42
Ramenstein
Difficulty: 9/11
B.P.M.: 20 mins/3 hours 50 mins

by Jack Hudson
jack-hudson.com

44
Smoked Haddock on the Water
Difficulty: 2/11
B.P.M.: 10 mins/15 mins
☺ ☺

by Cassandra Agazzi Brooks
cassandraagazzibrooks.co.uk

46
Ladle of Filth
Difficulty: 6/11
B.P.M.: 10 mins/25 mins

by Louise Zergaeng Pomeroy
louisezpomeroy.com

36
Mötley Stue
Difficulty: 3/11
B.P.M.: 10 mins/35 mins
Ⓥ Ⓥ
by Hattie Stewart
hattiestewart.com

38
ZZ Chop
Difficulty: 5/11
B.P.M.: 30 mins/40 mins
ⒼⒻ
by Yeji Yun
seeouterspace.com

40
Metallikatsu Curry
Difficulty: 8/11
B.P.M.: 10 mins/50 mins

by Bradley Jay
bradleyjay.co.uk

Extended Play

48
Primal Bream
Difficulty: 3/11
B.P.M.: 5 mins/20 mins
Ⓥ
by Paul Hill (Vagabond Tattoo)
iamvagabond.co.uk

50
Def Sheppard
Difficulty: 4/11
B.P.M.: 15 mins/1 hour 10 mins

by Mudrok
samuelmurdoch.co.uk

52
Limp Brisket
Difficulty: 8/11
B.P.M.: 10 mins/3 hours 40 mins

by Paul Layzell
layzellbros.com

Recipe Index—Desserts

Extended Play

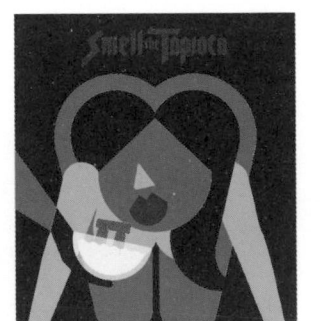

56
Iron Raisin
Difficulty: 4/11
B.P.M.: 1 hour/30 mins
Ⓥ Ⓟ
by Andy Baker
andy-baker.com

64
Nirvana Split
Difficulty: 4/11
B.P.M.: 40 mins/1 hour 10 mins
Ⓥ Ⓟ Ⓖ
by Patch D. Keyes
patchdkeyes.co.uk

66
Spinal Tapioca
Difficulty: 11/11
B.P.M.: 4 hours/20 mins
Ⓥ Ⓟ
by JMWL
jmwl.studio

68
Dire Dates
Difficulty: 6/11
B.P.M.: 20 mins/45 mins
Ⓥ Ⓟ
by Peter Stadden
peterstadden.co.uk

**58
Slayer Cake**
Difficulty: 8/11
B.P.M.: 45 mins/35 mins
ⓥ ℗
by Sam Taylor
samtaylorillustrator.com

**60
The Rolling Scones**
Difficulty: 2/11
B.P.M.: 15 mins/15 mins
ⓥ ℗
by Rob Flowers
robflowers.co.uk

**62
Smashing Pumpkin Pie**
Difficulty: 7/11
B.P.M.: 20 mins/1 hour 15 mins
ⓥ ℗
by Stuart Patience
stuartpatience.co.uk

**70
Sepultempura Fried Ice Cream**
Difficulty: 10/11
B.P.M.: 6 hours 10 mins/12 mins
ⓥ ℗
by Pete Sharp
petesharpart.com

**72
Judas Peach**
Difficulty: 3/11
B.P.M.: 10 mins/50 mins
ⓥ ℗
by Kristian Jones
kristian-jones.co.uk

**74
Whitesnaked Alaska**
Difficulty: 10/11
B.P.M.: 6 hours 30 mins/15 mins
ⓥ ℗
by Daniel Boyle
treatstudios.com

Extended Play

Dietary Information

Gluten-free—does not contain gluten

These dishes can easily be made without gluten. We recommend you check each ingredient though, as it's not unusual for items to unexpectedly have gluten in them. You can make these recipes gluten-free by doing the following:

Tofu Fighters: Swap the soy sauce for gluten-free soy sauce.
Beef Patty Smith: Swap the bread rolls for gluten-free bread rolls.
The Offspring Rolls: Swap the pastry wraps for rice wraps (although you won't be able to fry them), also swap the soy sauce for gluten-free soy sauce.
Mötley Stüe: Check the stock is gluten-free and swap the bread for gluten-free bread.
Ramenstein: Swap the ramen noodles for rice noodles and check the spices are made in a gluten-free environment.
Ladle of Filth: Check the stock is gluten-free.
Primal Bream: Check the spices are made in a gluten-free environment.
Def Sheppard: Check the stock is gluten-free.
Limp Brisket: Make sure the fajita mix and beef stock are gluten-free.
The Rolling Scones: Swap the flour with gluten-free flour.
Spinal Tapioca: The tapioca is gluten-free, but the cookies are not.
Sepultempura Fried Ice Cream: Swap the bread for gluten-free bread, and use gluten-free flour in place of the plain flour. Make sure the ice cream is gluten-free.
Judas Peach: Swap the plain flour for gluten-free flour and check the oats are gluten-free.
Whitesnaked Alaska: Use a gluten-free cake for the base, and ensure your ice cream is gluten-free.

Vegan—does not contain any animal product

You can make these recipes vegan by doing the following:

Tofu Fighters: Swap the honey for a vegan fruit nectar.
The Offspring Rolls: Swap the pastry wraps for rice wraps (although you can't fry them).

Extended Play

Setlist

Have a rock festival in your kitchen. In the official *Dark Side of the Spoon* setlist, every one of the 36 dishes is catered for. For the full *Dark Side of the Spoon* experience, scan the QR code below, or visit darksideofthespooncookbook.com. Warning: Some lyrics are explicit. Enjoy!

Extended Play

1. Fleetwood Mac—Go Your Own Way
2. Pink Floyd—Comfortably Numb
3. Foo Fighters—Learn To Fly
4. Patti Smith—Because The Night
5. Captain Beefheart—Observatory Crest
6. Suzi Quatro—Devil Gate Drive
7. Slipknot—Spit It Out
8. Status Quo—Rockin' All Over The World
9. The Offspring—Pretty Fly (For A White Guy)
10. Sum 41—Fat Lip

11. Sex Pistols—God Save The Queen
12. Mötley Crüe—Girls, Girls, Girls
13. ZZ Top—Sharp Dressed Man
14. Metallica—Master Of Puppets
15. Rammstein—Du Hast
16. Deep Purple—Smoke On The Water
17. Cradle of Filth—Tortured Soul Asylum
18. Primal Scream—Come Together
19. Def Leppard—When Love & Hate Collide
20. Limp Bizkit—Rollin' (Air Raid Vehicle)

21. Iron Maiden—Run To The Hills
22. Slayer—Angel Of Death
23. The Rolling Stones—You Can't Always Get What You Want
24. The Smashing Pumpkins—Ava Adore
25. Nirvana—Smells Like Teen Spirit
26. Spinal Tap—Stonehenge
27. Dire Straits—Sultans Of Swing
28. Sepultura—Troops Of Doom
29. Judas Priest—Ram It Down
30. Whitesnake—Here I Go Again

31. Bruce Springsteen—Born To Run
32. Korn—Freak On A Leash
33. Toto—Africa
34. Bachman-Turner Overdrive—You Ain't Seen Nothing Yet
35. Soundgarden—Black Hole Sun
36. Andrew W.K.—Party Hard

Outro

This book wouldn't be possible without the help of a huge number of people. We would like to say a big thank you to the following people for their support and contribution to the making of *Dark Side of the Spoon*:

Sophie Drysdale, Andrew Roff, Kathryn Colwell and the team at Laurence King Publishing Ltd. Björn Almqvist, Andy Baker, Katie Baxter, Joe Bichard, Daniel Boyle, Cassie Agazzi Brooks, Tom Bunker, Alex Campbell, Fran Carson, Ollie Clarke, Adam Cruft, Stewart Davies, Mary-Jay East, Andrew Ellis (and the Ellis family), Lee Faber, Ewen Farr, Will Finlay, Amy Fletcher, Rob Flowers, Rob Gill, Nic Hargreaves, Robert Hastings, Paul Hill, Jack Hudson, Harriet, Rona, Sue, Vicki and Warren Inniss, Anje Jager, Kristian Jones, Chris Kay, Jae Kerridge, Patch D. Keyes, Annemarieke Kloosterhof, Eve Lloyd Knight, Paul Layzell, Gary Lincoln, Joe Luxton, Mandy, Peter and Penny Miller, Alice Moloney, Rebecca Morris, Hadi Mukhtar, Sam Murdoch, Tom Murphy, Tom J. Newell, Laura Nickoll, Stuart Patience, Tom Peacock, Louise Zergaeng Pomeroy, Garret Power, Sam Ritchie, Matt Robinson, Nicolas Robinson, Lily Samengo-Turner, Pete Sharp, Joe Sparkes, Jessica Spencer, Richard and Sharon Stadden, Lucy Stehlik, Hattie Stewart, Sam Taylor, Edward Whittaker, Yeji Yun, Lynnie Zulu.

Extended Play

Dark Side of the Spoon Community

Keep updated with all things *Dark Side of the Spoon*. We'd love to hear from you!

W darksideofthespooncookbook.com

⊙ @dsotscookbook

🐦 @dsotscookbook

f facebook.com/dsotscookbook

If you enjoyed *Dark Side of the Spoon*, you might also want to check out our other cookbook *Rapper's Delight: The Hip Hop Cookbook*. See rappersdelightcookbook.com for more information.